Cubs Coloring and Activity Book

1st Edition Collectible

By Sara A. Miller and Jo Hershberger

CubsColoringBook.com

HawksNestPublishing.com

Hawk's Nest Publishing, LLC

Official Licensee -- Major League Baseball Player's Association
visit www.MLBPLAYERS.com, the Players Choice on the web.

Major League Baseball trademarks and copyrights are used with permission of
Major League Baseball Properties, Inc. MLB.com

ISBN-10: 0-9790872-6-0
ISBN-13: 978-0-9790872-6-4

Illustrations by
Scott Waddell
www.ScottWaddellFinearts.com

Cover Design and Interior Layout by
Matt Haas
www.MattHaas.com

Special thanks to Christina Adams, Barbara Epstein, and the Turi Family
for their contributions to the successful release of this book.

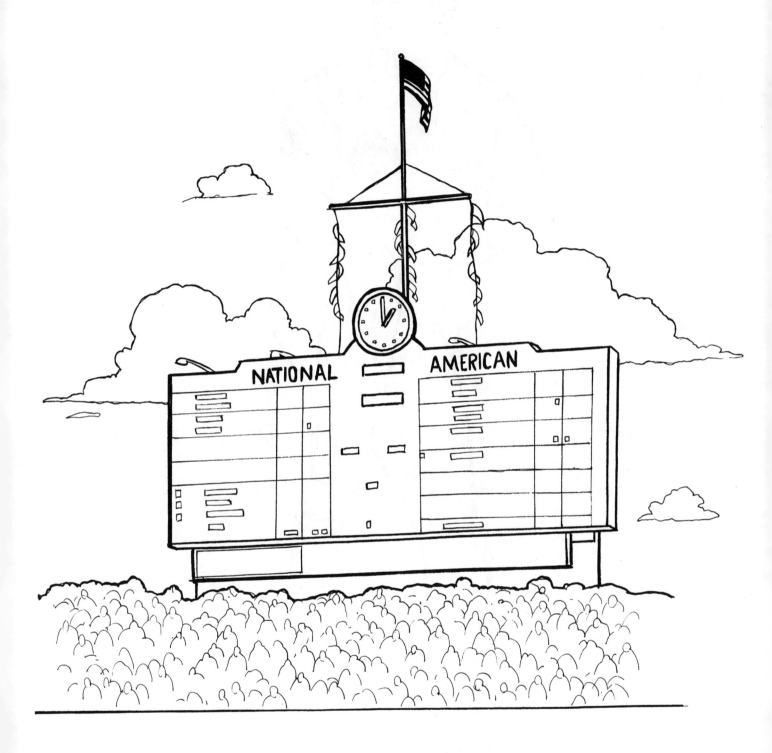

The historic scoreboard of Wrigley Field has welcomed fans to the ballpark since 1937.

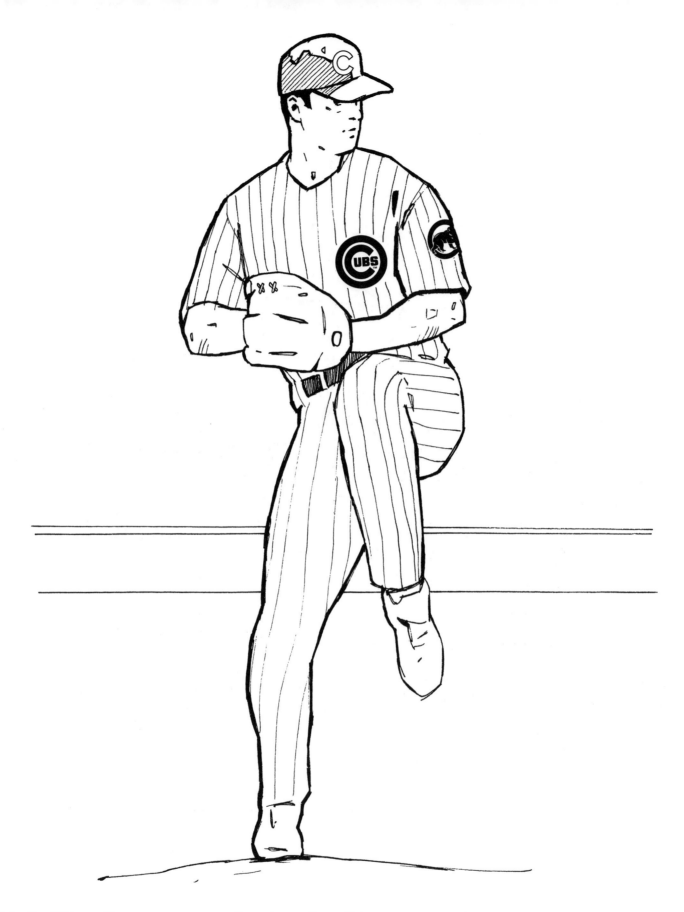

Rich Harden stares down the batter as he prepares to deliver his unpredictable ghost pitch.

Derrek Lee crushes another fastball into the bleachers for a home run and a lucky fan.

Use your knowledge about the 2008 *Cubs* team to solve the following crossword puzzle.

Crossword Puzzle 1

2008 *National League Central Division* Champions

Across

1 This player led the 2008 Cubs with home runs

3 This player started as a rookie in 2008 All-Star Game

5 This pitcher went from closer to starter in 2008

8 This starter pitched a no-hitter in September

9 This player was an LSU teammate of Theriot

11 This 6'5" player came from the Marlins in 2003

13 Fans sing this song after a Cubs victory (three words)

14 This Oakland Athletics ace joined Cubs staff in July

15 This former Cardinals player is now singing in the Cubs centerfield

Down

1 This rookie was a standout receiver with Notre Dame's Fighting Irish

2 The Cubs acquired this player from the Pirates in 2003

4 This player helped lead LSU to 2000 NCAA championship

6 This manager took Cubs to postseason two consecutive years

7 Fans who sit near the centerfield scoreboard (two words)

9 This player wears #1 on his jersey

10 This versatile Cub played at more different positions than any other teammate in 2008

12 This pitcher went from starter to closer in 2008

Use your knowledge about the 2008 *Cubs* team to solve the following crossword puzzle.

Crossword Puzzle 1

2008 *National League Central Division* Champions

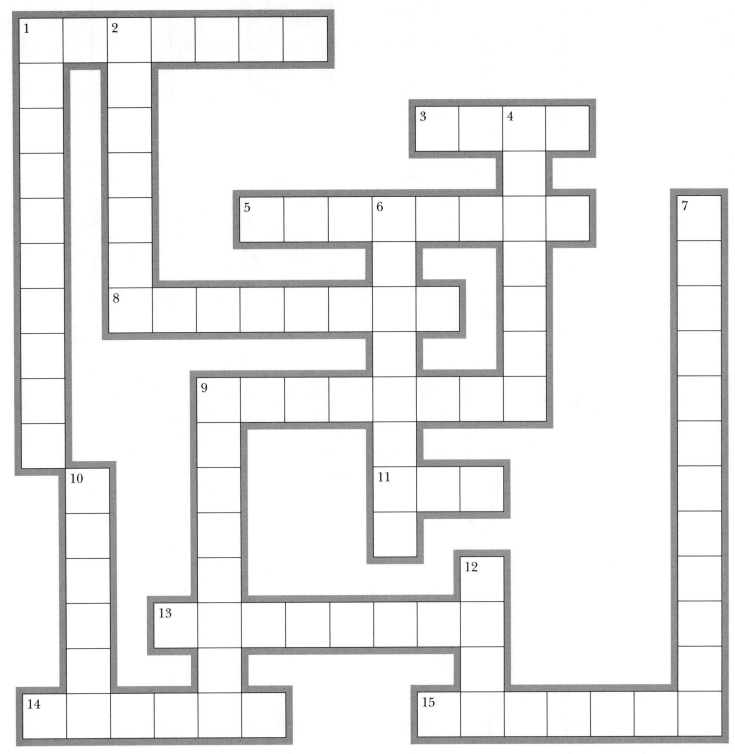

Solution is on page 53.

Connect-the-Dots #1

Connnect the dots to reveal what's on these pinstripes!

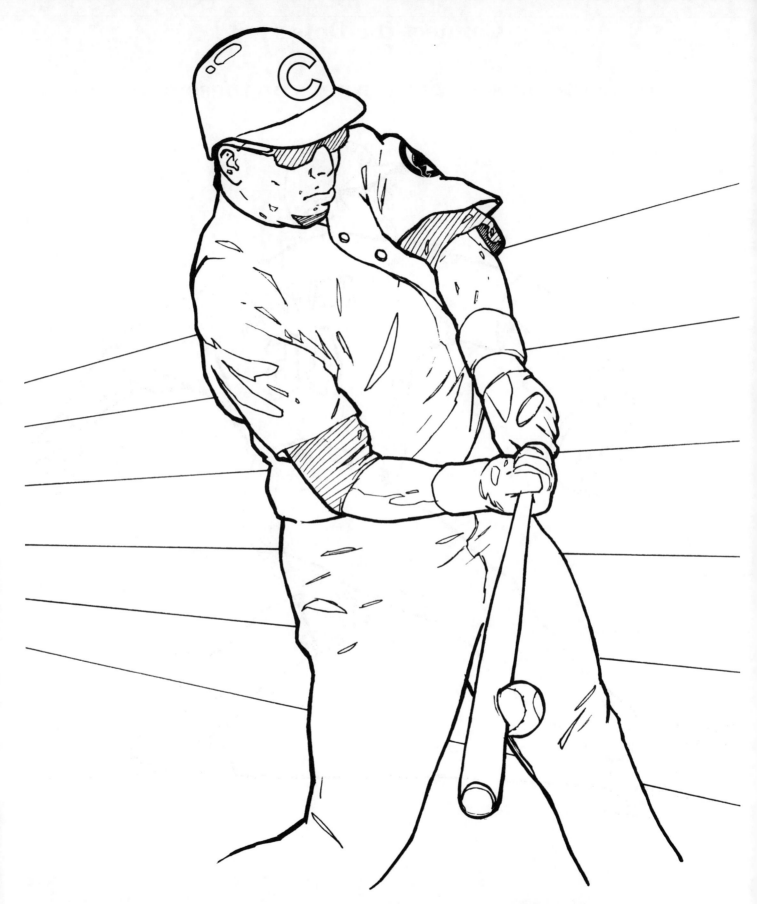

Aramis Ramirez connects on one of his 160 hits in the 2008 season.

Righthander Ryan Dempster throws a strike during one of his 17 wins in 2008.

Word Search #1
All-Time *Cubs* Favorites

```
Z A P T P D Z O I K B Y O T N A S O R R
G L O U F E O J W N B M A D D U X F R L
Z O B O W R L I M O K N S L A G L E M Z
R C Z S R A L M E S U D X S Z U U F P M
H K S H D L L R R W O D S B O A W G I E
R L J A I U Y P K A Z S V K S S R I F F
E C A A N Z N T L D V W E N N U A B B F
N S M S P D J A E L L Q R M D A G G Y I
K S U Z T P B M Q G B O F Z I Y B K B L
C C K T B M A E R N H F I X D R B C T C
U Y P L T H B A R V X E V K R M G A F T
B Q B K R E C U Y G L N L T A M W H Q U
Q Y M U Z E R E T A T W E S R E W J A S
U O D R B W D Y N V K O H L I N V N J Z
W N F E O B I E F O U R Z N G U W S C H
B K G D V L K M Y F F B P I B T C W P V
```

Try to find all the words contained in the list below: (Hint: Words may be found by looking up and down, across, or diagonally. Some words are even spelled backwards!)

BANKS	DURHAM	GRUDZIELANEK	ROOT	SOSA
BROWN	GIRARDI	HACK	SANDBERG	SUTCLIFFE
BUCKNER	GRACE	MADDUX	SANTO	SUTTER
DAWSON	GRIMES	MERKLE	SLAGLE	WILLIAMS

Solution is on page 53.

2008 *Cubs* Player Challenge
Cubs Roster effective November 1, 2009

No	PITCHERS	B	T	HT	WT	DOB
58	Jose Ascanio	R	R	6-0	170	05/02/85
48	Neal Cotts	L	L	6-1	200	03/25/80
46	Ryan Dempster	R	R	6-2	215	05/03/77
44	Chad Fox	R	R	6-3	215	09/03/70
57	Chad Gaudin	R	R	5-10	190	03/24/83
37	Angel Guzman	R	R	6-3	200	12/14/81
40	Rich Harden	L	R	6-1	195	11/30/81
22	Kevin Hart	R	R	6-4	220	12/29/82
53	Rich Hill	L	L	6-5	205	03/11/80
62	Bob Howry	L	R	6-5	220	08/04/73
30	Ted Lilly	L	L	6-1	190	01/04/76
49	Carlos Marmol	R	R	6-2	180	10/14/82
21	Jason Marquis	L	R	6-1	210	08/21/78
45	Sean Marshall	L	L	6-7	220	08/30/82
29	Jeff Samardzija	R	R	6-5	220	01/23/85
36	Randy Wells	R	R	6-5	235	08/28/82
34	Kerry Wood	R	R	6-5	210	06/16/77
43	Michael Wuertz	R	R	6-3	205	12/15/78
38	Carlos Zambrano	S	R	6-5	255	06/01/81
No	Catchers	B	T	HT	WT	DOB
24	Henry Blanco	R	R	5-11	220	08/29/71
55	Koyie Hill	S	R	6-0	190	03/09/79
18	Geovany Soto	R	R	6-1	225	01/20/83
No	Infielders	B	T	HT	WT	DOB
5	Ronny Cedeno	R	R	6-0	180	02/02/83
7	Mark DeRosa	R	R	6-1	205	02/26/75
17	Mike Fontenot	L	R	5-8	170	06/09/80
6	Micah Hoffpauir	L	L	6-3	215	03/01/80
25	Derrek Lee	R	R	6-5	245	09/06/75
16	Aramis Ramirez	R	R	6-1	215	06/25/78
2	Ryan Theriot	R	R	5-11	175	12/07/79
33	Daryle Ward	L	L	6-2	240	06/27/75
No	Outfielders	B	T	HT	WT	DOB
15	Jim Edmonds	L	L	6-1	210	06/27/70
1	Kosuke Fukudome	L	R	6-0	185	04/26/77
9	Reed Johnson	R	R	5-10	180	12/08/76
20	Felix Pie	L	L	6-2	170	02/08/85
12	Alfonso Soriano	R	R	6-1	180	01/07/76

2008 *Cubs* Player Challenge

Use the names on the *Cubs* roster to fill in the correct players who made these accomplishments

1. _____ won the 2005 National League batting title.

2. Former starting ace _____ battled through injuries and long rehab sessions to become the Cubs closer in 2008.

3. _____ and _____ were a great defensive tandem in centerfield in 2008.

4. _____ had a total of 111 RBI in 2008.

5. After joining the Cubs in July 2008, _____ compiled a sparkling ERA in 12 starts.

6. Former LSU teammates _____ and _____ each batted over .300 in 2008.

7. _____ was the youngest Cubs player in franchise history to play in a Major League Baseball All-Star Game in 2004.

8. Pitchers _____ and _____ each had 17 wins in 2008.

9.In 2008 _____ was named an All-Star during his first full season.

10. _____ hit 29 home runs as the Cubs leadoff hitter in 2008.

Solution is on page 54.

Use your knowledge about *Cubs* trivia to solve the following crossword puzzle.

Crossword Puzzle 2 - *Cubs* Trivia

Across

1 Cubs manager, Herman _____ , said "Chicago Cubs fans are the greatest fans in baseball. They've got to be."

4 A black cat strolling across Shea Stadium was one of a few strange incidents that occurred in 1969 when the Cubs let a ____ game lead slip away.

6 Columnist George Will said that Cubs fans are "90% _____ tissue."

8 _____ was the pitcher on the mound when the Steve Bartman incident occurred. (two words)

9 On April 29, 1987, _____ hit for the cycle.

11 Cubs pitcher, Mordecai Brown, had only _____ fingers on his pitching hand.

13 1962's opening day shortstop was _____ White. He took over when Banks moved to first base.

14 Greg Maddux was named a _____ winner in 1992. (two words)

15 Leon Durham let a ground ball go through his legs during game _____ of the 1984 National League Championship Series.

Down

2 Kerry Wood was named _____ of the Year in 1998.

3 Carlos Zambrano pitched a no hitter against the Milwaukee _____ on September 14, 2008.

5 Ron Santo would _____ and click his heels together following a Cubs win.

6 Hippo Vaughn was the _____ champion in 1918 and 1919. (two words)

7 Bill Dahlen holds the Cubs franchise record for the longest _____ streak, set in 1894.

10 The last Cubs manager with over 100 losses in a single season was _____.

12 The Cubs call _____ Park Stadium in Mesa, AZ home during spring training.

Use your knowledge about *Cubs* trivia to solve the following crossword puzzle.

Crossword Puzzle 2 - *Cubs* Trivia

Solution is on page 54.

"Big Z" shows the form that has made him a legend with Cubs fans.

Geovany Soto hunkers down to make a play on Dodgers catcher Russell Martin at the plate.

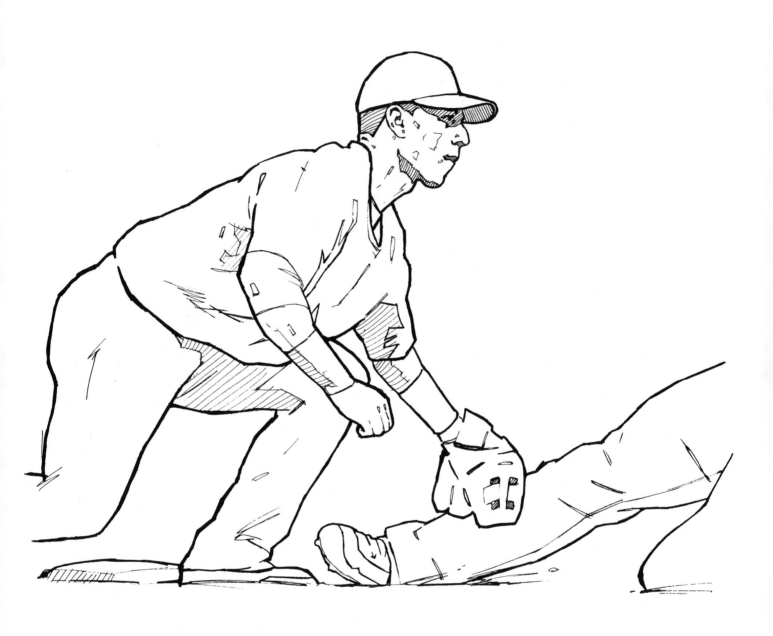

Ronny Cedeno makes the tag at second base to start a double play.

Ball or strike? Fair or Foul? Safe or Out? Usually, the umpires have to make the tough decisions, but now... YOU MAKE THE CALL!

Here's the situation...

It's the 5th inning and Ted Lilly is sitting on a comfortable 12-0 lead for the Cubs over the Pittsburgh Pirates. There are two outs with Pirates player Adam LaRoche on first base. Wanting to give his starter some rest, Lou Piniella decides to pull Lilly and relieve him with Neal Cotts.

Cotts comes into the game and immediately picks off LaRoche at first for the third out, without even throwing a pitch. Carlos Marmol then enters the game to pitch the 6th inning and the rest of the game. Cubs win, 12-2. Who gets the win?

Solution is on page 54.

Solve the *Cubs* Scramble

Unscramble the letters below to reveal *Cubs* words or phrases:

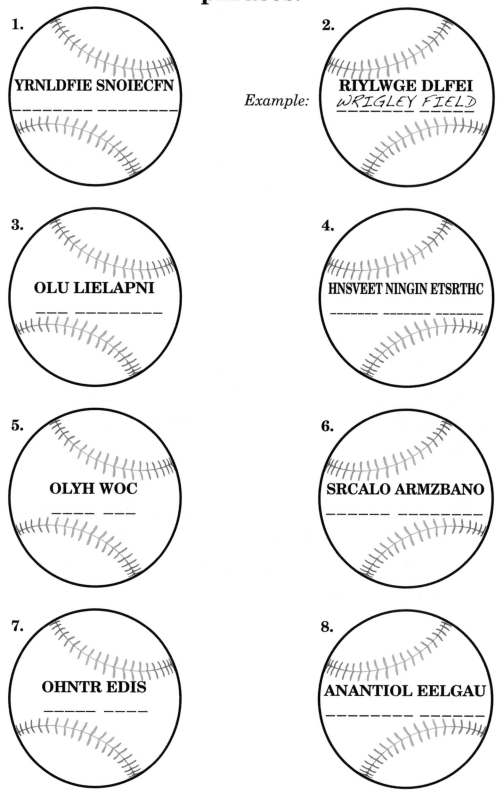

1.
YRNLDFIE SNOIECFN

_____ _____

2.
RIYLWGE DLFEI

Example: WRIGLEY FIELD

3.
OLU LIELAPNI

___ _____

4.
HNSVEET NINGIN ETSRTHC

_____ _____ _____

5.
OLYH WOC

____ ___

6.
SRCALO ARMZBANO

_____ _____

7.
OHNTR EDIS

_____ ____

8.
ANANTIOL EELGAU

_____ _____

Solution is on page 55.

Alfonso Soriano fires up the fans with a steal to get into scoring position for Mark DeRosa.

Cubs Nicknames Challenge

Match these famous Cubs nicknames to the players (from the past and present) that appear on the next page:

| "Mr. Cub" | "The Hawk" | "The Riot" | "Old Sarge" |

| "Ginger" | "Bull" | "The Lip" | "The Eck" |

| "Bonehead" | "Ryno" | "Pizza" |

| "Slammin' Sammy" | "Fonzie" | "Red Baron" | "Mr. Home Run" |

| "Billy Buck" | "The Human Rally Killer" | "El Toro" | "Popeye" |

Cubs Nicknames Challenge

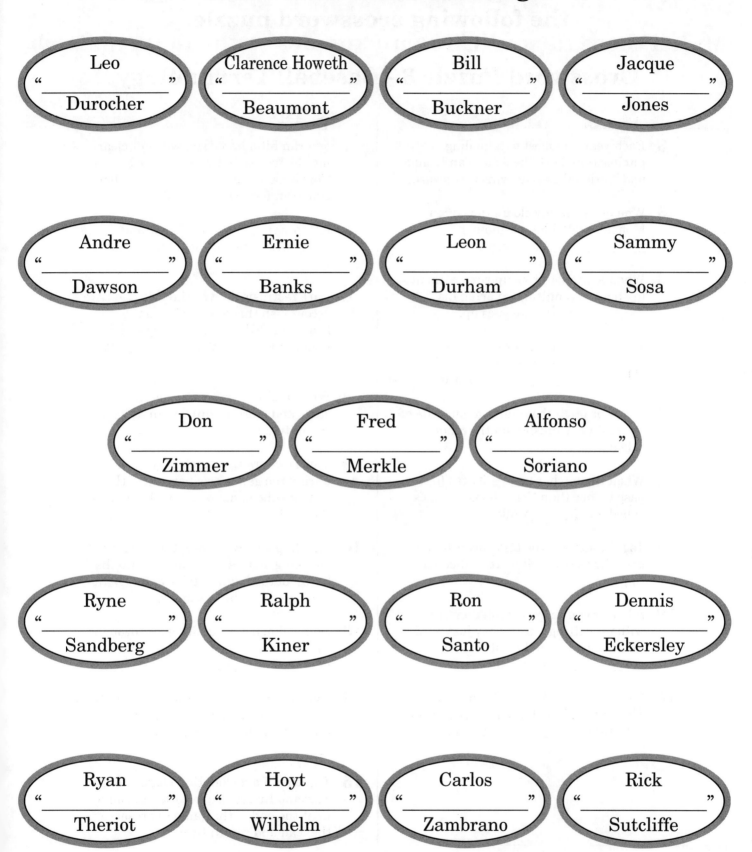

Leo
" _____ "
Durocher

Clarence Howeth
" _____ "
Beaumont

Bill
" _____ "
Buckner

Jacque
" _____ "
Jones

Andre
" _____ "
Dawson

Ernie
" _____ "
Banks

Leon
" _____ "
Durham

Sammy
" _____ "
Sosa

Don
" _____ "
Zimmer

Fred
" _____ "
Merkle

Alfonso
" _____ "
Soriano

Ryne
" _____ "
Sandberg

Ralph
" _____ "
Kiner

Ron
" _____ "
Santo

Dennis
" _____ "
Eckersley

Ryan
" _____ "
Theriot

Hoyt
" _____ "
Wilhelm

Carlos
" _____ "
Zambrano

Rick
" _____ "
Sutcliffe

Solution is on page 55.

Use your knowledge about baseball terminology to solve the following crossword puzzle.

Crossword Puzzle 3 - Baseball Terminology

Across

3 Each year, the most outstanding pitcher from both the American League and National League wins this award.

5 Whenever Manny clears the Green Monster wall, he's hit another _____. (two words)

6 When a pitcher gives up runs without his team committing an error, his _____ run average goes up.

7 When there's a runner on first, the second basemen and shortstop will try to turn a _____. (two words)

11 A slower pitch that starts at one side of the plate but finishes on the other is called a _____.

12 When the pitcher gives a batter first base rather than risk a home run, it's called an _____ walk.

16 Ted Williams is the last player to have one of these over .400. It's called batting _____.

18 A batter can score a runner on third without getting a hit. They just need to hit it deep into the outfield for a _____. (two words)

19 Lefties have a great one to first base. They'll try to catch the runner sleeping with their _____. (2 words)

Down

1 You can hit a home run without clearing the fences, but you'd better be fast. This is called an _____ home run. (three words)

2 Nolan Ryan, Pedro Martinez, and Roger Clemens did this to many batters.

4 Carl Yastrzemski was the last player to accomplish this feat. He led the league in RBI, batting average, and home runs to win the _____. (two words)

8 When a pitcher starts his motion, then stops and tries to throw to first, he has committed a _____.

9 This is where the bench players sit during the game, or where the DH watches the game while his team is in the field.

10 This happens when a batter, instead of swinging, moves his hand up onto the barrel of the bat and tries to nudge the ball up one of the baselines.

13 Oops! When a grounder goes through the shortstop's legs or an outfielder muffs a fly ball, they get an _____.

14 Once you've reached first base, you can take a few steps towards second before the next pitch. This is called a _____.

15 Jonathan Papelbon, Eric Gagne, and Mariano Rivera are experts at coming in at the end of the game to preserve the lead and record these.

17 This play is risky. When the manager sends the runner from third and the batter lays down a bunt, it's called a suicide _____.

Crossword Puzzle 3 - Baseball Terminology

Solution is on page 56.

Maze #1

Master the maze to help Rich Harden throw a strike to Geovany Soto.

Solution is on page 56.

Aramis Ramirez slams one of his many doubles into center field to score two runners.

International Game

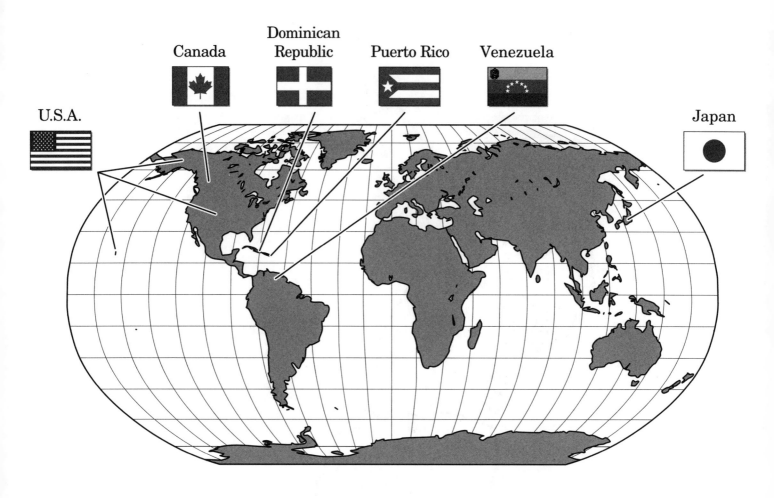

Baseball is an international game. Match these *Cubs* players with their countries of origin. Write each player's name on the next page, below the flag of the country where he was born.

Ryan Theriot
Geovany Soto
Reed Johnson
Kosuke Fukudome
Mark DeRosa
Ronny Cedeno
Jim Edmonds
Daryle Ward
Alfonso Soriano

Mike Fontenot
Derrek Lee
Aramis Ramirez
Kerry Wood
Rich Harden
Jason Marquis
Ryan Dempster
Carlos Zambrano
Ted Lilly

International Game

Write each player's name from the previous page below the flag of the country where he was born:

U.S.A.

Example: *Ryan Theriot*

_____

_____

_____

_____

_____

_____

Dominican Republic

_____

_____

Canada

_____

Puerto Rico

_____

Japan

_____

Venezuela

_____

_____

Solution is on page 57.

Word Search #2
2008 *National League Central Division* Champions

```
G E F B H O T O S D O G K Y I N E G U E
Q Z L R N Q B O M D N J W Q Q X N A K L
S J V O W O N O E A A A F B P P Y A V X
E X P O M E O M Z Y R A Z Q P P U D H R
D F D H D R P D T D B R A C O L I U D F
Y O K E W S A W A T M G A U D I N U S U
T N C U T I L M N C A H A S O R E D N K
O T Q E O U X R J Y Z B W O O D H L O U
I E R B B Q S A X X B E Q L F M O O S D
R N R Q C R D P O M C T D A P Z E T N O
E O L A K A N N D R R X T M V L E C H M
H T V I M M A A W A N P M M O S L S O E
T K H W L I N E D R A H U V D N B J J V
H J B B R L R Z L U F N F M G D D E P K
T N F O T F Y E W L T P Y S M X V S U K
Z D S N L N S H Z Z R I M K M X G X V S
```

Try to find all the words contained in the list below: (Hint: Words may be found by looking up and down, across, or diagonally. Some words are even spelled backwards!)

CEDENO	FONTENOT	JOHNSON	MARQUIS	THERIOT
DEMPSTER	FUKUDOME	LEE	RAMIREZ	WARD
DEROSA	GAUDIN	LILLY	SORIANO	WOOD
EDMONDS	HARDEN	MARMOL	SOTO	ZAMBRANO

Solution is on page 57.

Mike Fontenot holds his ground at second base for the first out of a double play.

Closer Kerry Wood zings a strike over the plate during one of his 24 saves in 2008.

Ball or strike? Fair or Foul? Safe or Out? Usually, the umpires have to make the tough decisions, but now... YOU MAKE THE CALL!

Here's the situation...

It's the bottom of the 3rd inning with one out. Mark DeRosa is up to bat with Alfonso Soriano on first. DeRosa hits a line drive to Milwaukee Brewers first baseman, Prince Fielder, who dives but can only trap the ball, not catch it.

Soriano, believing Fielder caught the ball, heads back to first base. Fielder tags first base and then tags Soriano, who is back standing on first base. What will the umpire call?

Solution is on page 58.

Retired Numbers at *Wrigley Field* Matching Game

Match the famous the player below with the retired number that they wore on the ball field. Enter the name of the player below the uniform containing their number on the next page.

Ernie Banks	• Shortstop/1st Base • Elected to National Baseball Hall of Fame in 1977 • Granted 1967 Lou Gehrig Memorial Award • 11 time All Star selection • Holds the Cubs record for 2528 games played
Ron Santo	• 3rd base • 5 time Gold Glove winner • 9 time All Star selection • Batted in 1331 runs during career • Became Cubs commentator for WGN in 1990
Billy Williams	• Outfield • Elected to National Baseball Hall of Fame in 1987 • 6 time All Star selection • Led the MLB in runs and hits in 1970 • 1961 Rookie of the Year
Ryne Sandberg	• 3rd Base/2nd Base • Elected to National Baseball Hall of Fame in 2005 • 9 time Gold Glove winner • 10 time All Star selection • Led National League in home runs in 1990

Retired Numbers at *Wrigley Field* Matching Game

_____

_____

_____

_____

Solution is on page 58.

Use your knowledge about *Cubs* history to solve the following crossword puzzle.

Crossword Puzzle 4 - Down Memory Lane

Across

1 Future Hall of Famer who pitched two different stints with the Cubs

4 His #26 is now retired

6 "Mr. Cub" who always said, "Let's play two!"

7 Hall-of-Famer who manages the Cubs Peoria farm team

8 Nicknamed "Rebel"

9 Three-fingered Hall of Fame pitcher

11 Managed the 1908 World Series champions

12 Catcher whose name could be sung to "The Ballad of Davy Crockett"

14 National League MVP in 1945

15 Hit for the cycle in May 1993

Down

2 Called "The Hawk"

3 New York Yankees manager who started his playing career with Cubs

5 Known as the "Red Baron"

7 Organist played theme from "The Godfather" each time he went to bat

8 Second baseman & Rookie of the Year in 1962

10 Hit a career-high 41 home runs in 1954

11 Started the tradition of singing "Take Me Out To The Ball Game" during seventh-inning stretch

13 Played in all seven games of 1945 World Series

Crossword Puzzle 4 - Down Memory Lane

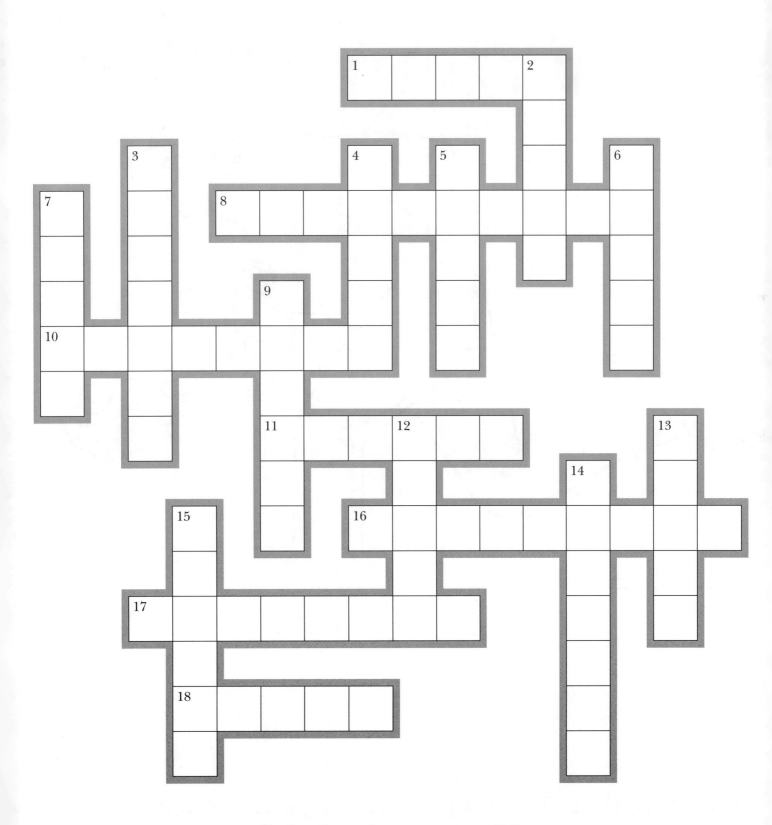

Solution is on page 58.

Shortstop Ryan Theriot plugs a hole in the infield as he scoops up a grounder.

Lefty Ted Lilly freezes a batter with a fastball on his way to another win.

Word Search #3
You'll find all of these around *Wrigley Field!*

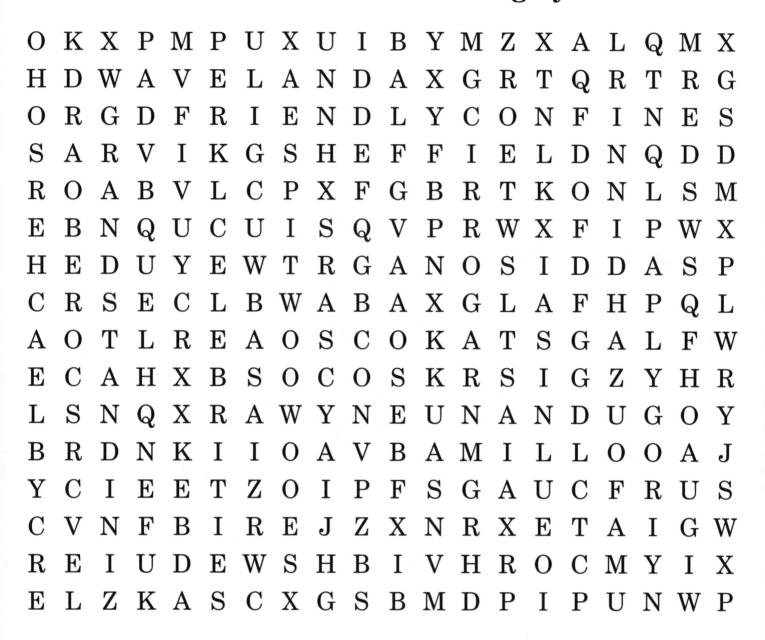

```
O K X P M P U X U I B Y M Z X A L Q M X
H D W A V E L A N D A X G R T Q R T R G
O R G D F R I E N D L Y C O N F I N E S
S A R V I K G S H E F F I E L D N Q D D
R O A B V L C P X F G B R T K O N L S M
E B N Q U C U I S Q V P R W X F I P W X
H E D U Y E W T R G A N O S I D D A S P
C R S E C L B W A B A X G L A F H P Q L
A O T L R E A O S C O K A T S G A L F W
E C A H X B S O C O S K R S I G Z Y H R
L S N Q X R A W Y N E U N A N D U G O Y
B R D N K I I O A V B A M I L L O O A J
Y C I E E T Z O I P F S G A U C F R U S
C V N F B I R E J Z X N R X E T A I G W
R E I U D E W S H B I V H R O C M Y I X
E L Z K A S C X G S B M D P I P U N W P
```

Try to find all the words contained in the list below: (Hint: Words may be found by looking up and down, across, or diagonally. Some words are even spelled backwards!)

ADDISON	CELEBRITIES	FLAGS	LAKEVIEW	SINGING
BLEACHERS	CLARK	FRIENDLY CONFINES	ROOFTOP	WAVELAND
BRICK	FANS	GRANDSTAND	SCOREBOARD	WIN
CARAY	EAMUS CATULI	IVY	SHEFFIELD	WOOWOO

Solution is on page 59.

Maze #2

Master the maze to help Aramis Ramirez send the ball to the fan in the upper deck!

Solution is on page 59.

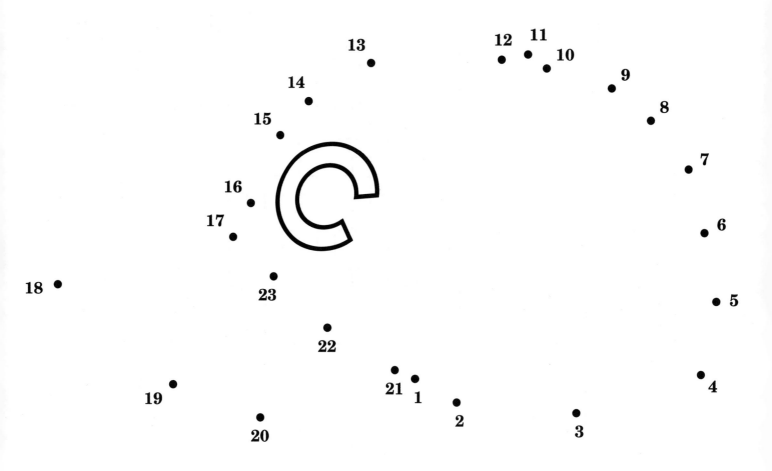

Worn by young and old, this is the sign of a true *Cubs* fan.

Carlos Zambrano rejoices after pitching the game of his a life, a no-hitter on Sept. 15, 2008.

Manager Lou Piniella stays focused as he guides his team toward another win.

Cubs Record Breakers - An Honors Quiz for Die-Hard Fans
Test Your *Cubs* Knowledge by entering the name of the player who holds the *Cubs* record below:

Most Hits in a Season _____

Most Stolen Bases in a Season _____

Most RBI with the Cubs _____

Most Home Runs with the Cubs _____

Most At Bats with the Cubs _____

Lowest ERA with the Cubs _____

Most Wins in a Season _____

Most Saves in a Season _____

Most Strikeouts with the Cubs _____

Most Strikeouts in a Season _____

Solution is on page 60.

Mark DeRosa backs up against the ivy to snag a fly ball.

Henry Blanco gets a high five from Ryan Theriot after hitting a home run.

Use your knowledge about *Cubs* history to solve the following crossword puzzle.

Crossword Puzzle 5 - *Cubs* History

Across

4 Park built for the Cubs in 1914.

8 This Cubs outfielder saved an American flag from burning in 1976?

9 How many times has the Major League Baseball All-Star Game been played at Wrigley Field?

10 The last Cubs pitcher to win 20 games in a season.

11 Umpire who ruined Pappas' perfect game.

13 Pitched a perfect no-hitter against the Cubs in 1965.

15 Lou Piniella's nickname (two words).

16 First official night game at Wrigley Field was played on _____ 9, 1988.

18 Which catcher from the Cardinals sent Carlos Zambrano a pair of shin guards?

Down

1 Andre Dawson's nickname.

2 He left his job at WGN to become manager of the Cubs in 1960.

3 Cubs hall-of-famer drafted by the Phillies in 1978.

5 What was the original name of Chicago's National League team (two words)?

6 Kosuke Fukudome's jersey bears this number, once worn by Jose Cardenal.

7 "Hey, hey" broadcaster.

8 Opponent for the first official night game at Wrigley Field.

12 Played quarterback at the University of Pennsylvania.

14 How many times have the Cubs been in the post-season?

15 How many ballparks have the Cubs called home?

17 The Cubs haven't won a World Series because of the curse of this animal.

Use your knowledge about *Cubs* history to solve the following crossword puzzle.

Crossword Puzzle 5 - *Cubs* History

Solution is on page 60.

Reliever Carlos Marmol fires his signature fastball for a strike.

Ball or strike? Fair or Foul? Safe or Out? Usually, the umpires have to make the tough decisions, but now... YOU MAKE THE CALL!

Here's the situation...

In the bottom of the 6th inning at Wrigley Field, the Cubs are trailing the Philadelphia Phillies 6-4. Phillies pitcher, Cole Hamels, is on the mound when Alfonso Soriano hits a flare over Hamels' head. Hamels removes his glove and tosses it in the air to knock the ball down. The glove makes contact and the ball lands near the the mound, as Soriano slides into third.

What will the umpire rule?

Solution is on page 60.

Kosuke Fukudome acknowledges the cheers of *Cubs* fans after making a diving catch.

Fill in the blanks
Learn more about Chicago, home of the *Cubs*

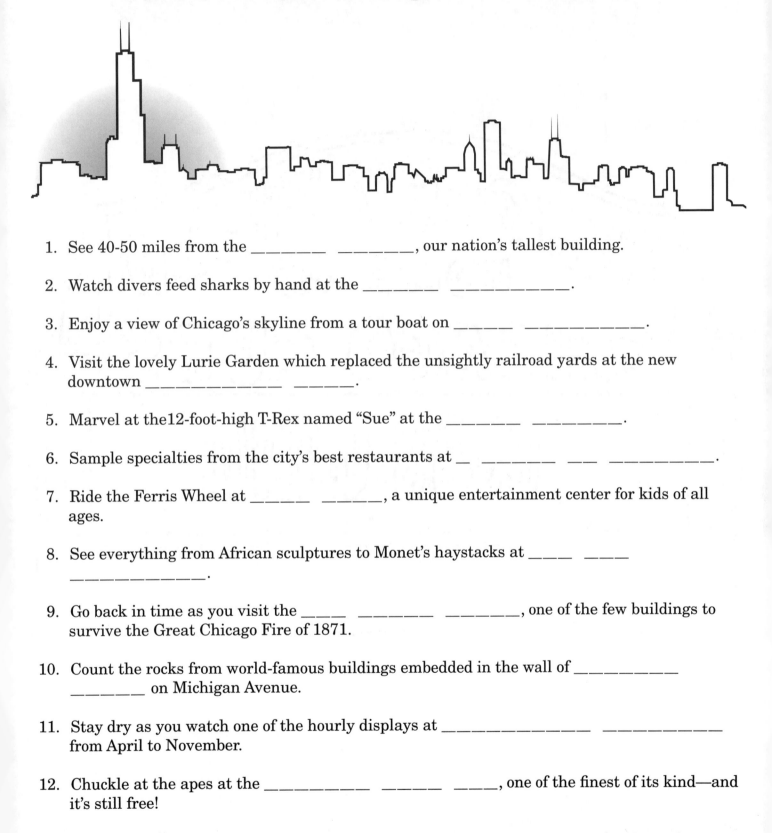

1. See 40-50 miles from the _____ _____, our nation's tallest building.

2. Watch divers feed sharks by hand at the _____ _____.

3. Enjoy a view of Chicago's skyline from a tour boat on _____ _____.

4. Visit the lovely Lurie Garden which replaced the unsightly railroad yards at the new downtown _____ _____.

5. Marvel at the 12-foot-high T-Rex named "Sue" at the _____ _____.

6. Sample specialties from the city's best restaurants at _ _____ ___ _____.

7. Ride the Ferris Wheel at _____ _____, a unique entertainment center for kids of all ages.

8. See everything from African sculptures to Monet's haystacks at ____ ____ _____.

9. Go back in time as you visit the ____ _____ _____, one of the few buildings to survive the Great Chicago Fire of 1871.

10. Count the rocks from world-famous buildings embedded in the wall of _____ _____ on Michigan Avenue.

11. Stay dry as you watch one of the hourly displays at _____ _____ from April to November.

12. Chuckle at the apes at the _____ _____ ____, one of the finest of its kind—and it's still free!

Solution is on page 60.

The Northsiders are in the win column again. What could be better?

Solutions to Puzzles
Crossword Puzzle 1, page 5
2008 *National League Central Division* Champions

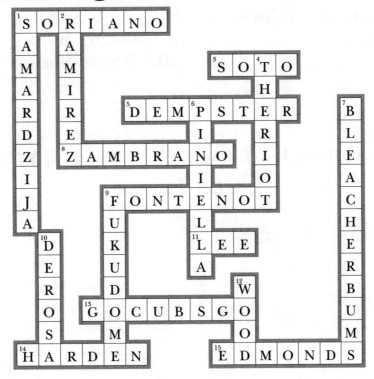

Solution to Word Search #1, page 9:
All-Time *Cubs* Favorites

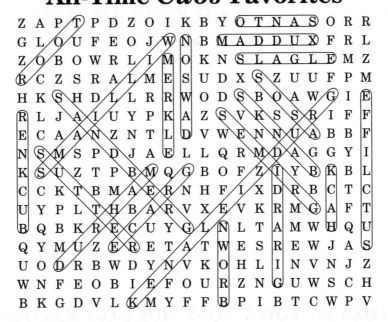

Try to find all the words contained in the list below: (Hint: Words may be found by looking up and down, across, or diagonally. Some words are even spelled backwards!)

BANKS	DURHAM	GRUDZIELANEK	ROOT	SOSA
BROWN	GIRARDI	HACK	SANDBERG	SUTCLIFFE
BUCKNER	GRACE	MADDUX	SANTO	SUTTER
DAWSON	GRIMES	MERKLE	SLAGLE	WILLIAMS

Solution to *Cubs* Player Challenge, page 11

1. Derrek Lee
2. Kerry Wood
3. Reed Johnson and Jim Edmonds
4. Aramis Ramirez
5. Rich Harden

6. Ryan Theriot and Mike Fontenot
7. Carlos Zambrano
8. Ryan Dempster and Ted Lilly
9. Geovany Soto
10. Alfonso Soriano

Solution to Crossword Puzzle 2, page 13
Cubs Trivia

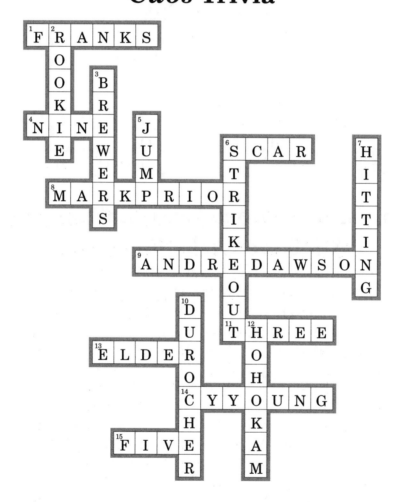

Solution to You Make the Call #1, page 17

The win would go to Cotts since Lilly didn't pitch five full innings and the lead didn't change while Marmol was pitching.

Solution to solve the *Cubs* Scramble, page 18

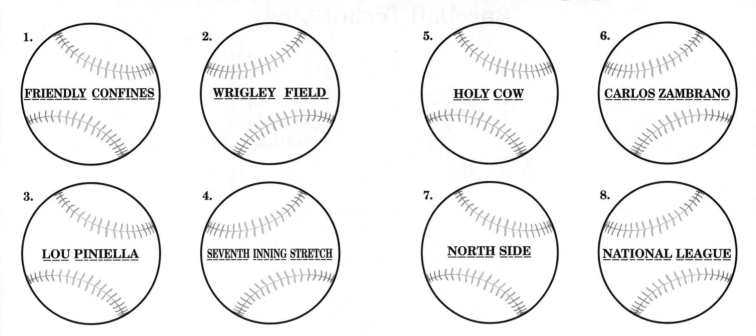

1. FRIENDLY CONFINES
2. WRIGLEY FIELD
5. HOLY COW
6. CARLOS ZAMBRANO
3. LOU PINIELLA
4. SEVENTH INNING STRETCH
7. NORTH SIDE
8. NATIONAL LEAGUE

Solution to solve the *Cubs* Nicknames, page 21

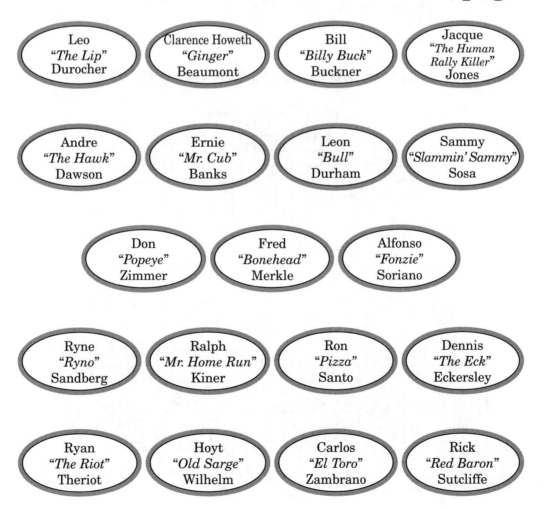

Leo *"The Lip"* Durocher

Clarence Howeth *"Ginger"* Beaumont

Bill *"Billy Buck"* Buckner

Jacque *"The Human Rally Killer"* Jones

Andre *"The Hawk"* Dawson

Ernie *"Mr. Cub"* Banks

Leon *"Bull"* Durham

Sammy *"Slammin' Sammy"* Sosa

Don *"Popeye"* Zimmer

Fred *"Bonehead"* Merkle

Alfonso *"Fonzie"* Soriano

Ryne *"Ryno"* Sandberg

Ralph *"Mr. Home Run"* Kiner

Ron *"Pizza"* Santo

Dennis *"The Eck"* Eckersley

Ryan *"The Riot"* Theriot

Hoyt *"Old Sarge"* Wilhelm

Carlos *"El Toro"* Zambrano

Rick *"Red Baron"* Sutcliffe

Solution to Crossword Puzzle 3, page 23
Baseball Terminology

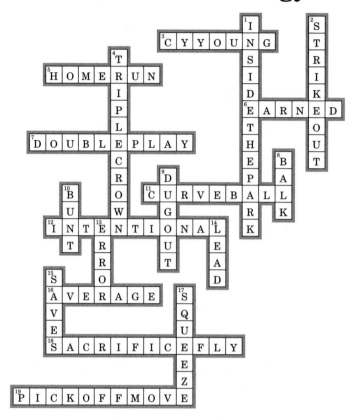

Solution to Maze 1, page 24

Solution to International Game, page 27

U.S.A.

Ryan Theriot
Derrek Lee
Mark DeRosa
Reed Johnson
Jim Edmonds
Daryle Ward
Mike Fontenot
Ted Lilly
Jason Marquis
Kerry Wood

Canada

Ryan Dempster
Rich Harden

Puerto Rico

Geovany Soto

Japan

Kosuke Fukudome

Dominican Republic

Alfonso Soriano
Aramis Ramirez

Venezuela

Ronny Cedeno
Carlos Zambrano

Solution to Word Search #2, page 28
2008 *National League Central Division* Champions

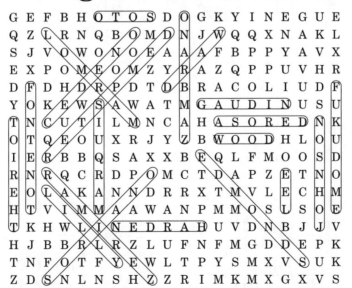

Try to find all the words contained in the list below: (Hint: Words may be found by looking up and down, across, or diagonally. Some words are even spelled backwards!)

CEDENO	FONTENOT	JOHNSON	MARQUIS	THERIOT
DEMPSTER	FUKUDOME	LEE	RAMIREZ	WARD
DEROSA	GAUDIN	LILLY	SORIANO	WOOD
EDMONDS	HARDEN	MARMOL	SOTO	ZAMBRANO

Solution to You Make the Call #2, page 31

DeRosa is out, removing the force out against Soriano, who is safe. Soriano was not forced at the time he was tagged and since he was touching first base, he is safe. Had Fielder tagged Soriano first and then tagged first base, it would have been a double play.

Solution to *Wrigley Field* Retired Numbers, page 33

Ron Santo   Ernie Banks   Ryne Sandberg   Billy Williams

Solution to Crossword Puzzle 4, page 35
Down Memory Lane

Solution to Word Search #3, page 38
You'll find all of these around *Wrigley Field!*

O K X P M P U X U I B Y M Z X A L Q M X
H D W A V E L A N D A X G R T Q R T R G
O R G D F R I E N D L Y C O N F I N E S
S A R V I K G S H E F F I E L D N Q D D
R O A B V L C P X F G B R T K O N L S M
E B N Q U C U I S Q V P R W X F I P W X
H E D U Y E W T R G A N O S I D D A S P
C R S E C L B W A B A X G L A F H P Q L
A O T L R E A O S C O K A T S G A L F W
E C A H X B S O C O S K R S I G Z Y H R
L A N Q X R A W Y N E U N A N D U G O Y
B R D N K I I O A V B A M I L L O O A J
Y C I E E T Z O I P F S G A U C F R U S
C V N F B I R E J Z X N R X E T A I G W
R E I U D E W S H B I V H R O C M Y I X
E L Z K A S C X G S B M D P I P U N W P

Try to find all the words contained in the list below: (Hint: Words may be found by looking up and down, across, or diagonally. Some words are even spelled backwards!)

ADDISON	CELEBRITIES	FLAGS	LAKEVIEW	SINGING
BLEACHERS	CLARK	FRIENDLY CONFINES	ROOFTOP	WAVELAND
BRICK	FANS	GRANDSTAND	SCOREBOARD	WIN
CARAY	EAMUS CATULI	IVY	SHEFFIELD	WOOWOO

Solution to Maze #2, page 39

Solution to solve the *Cubs* records, page 43

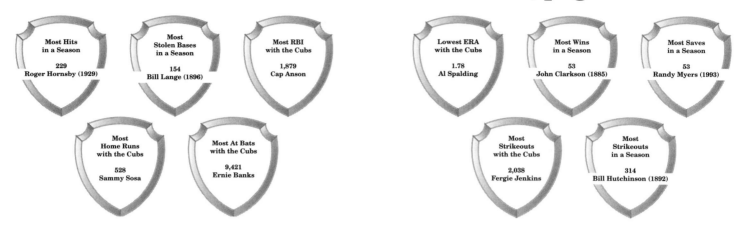

Most Hits in a Season — 229 — Roger Hornsby (1929)

Most Stolen Bases in a Season — 154 — Bill Lange (1896)

Most RBI with the Cubs — 1,879 — Cap Anson

Lowest ERA with the Cubs — 1.78 — Al Spalding

Most Wins in a Season — 53 — John Clarkson (1885)

Most Saves in a Season — 53 — Randy Myers (1993)

Most Home Runs with the Cubs — 528 — Sammy Sosa

Most At Bats with the Cubs — 9,421 — Ernie Banks

Most Strikeouts with the Cubs — 2,038 — Fergie Jenkins

Most Strikeouts in a Season — 314 — Bill Hutchinson (1892)

Solution to Crossword Puzzle 5, page 47
Cubs History

Solution to You Make the Call #3, page 49

Soriano will be awarded three bases on the play as the ball is not dead. Soriano could have even tried to advance home, but it would have been at his own risk.

Solution to Fill in the blanks, page 51

1. Sears Tower
2. Shedd Aquarium
3. Lake Michigan
4. Millenium Park
5. Field Museum
6. A Taste of Chicago
7. Navy Pier
8. The Art Institute
9. Old Water Tower
10. Tribune Tower
11. Buckingham Fountain
12. Lincoln Park Zoo

We hope that you enjoyed the first edition of the
Chicago Cubs Coloring and Activity Book!

Please contact us with questions or comments at:

Hawk's Nest Publishing LLC
84 Library Street
Mystic, CT 06355
www.HawksNestPublishing.com

Books for the Young and Young at Heart...

To order additional copies of this book:

Phone

Pathway Book Service
800-345-6665 or 603-357-0236

Web

www.CubsColoringBook.com

Mail

Hawk's Nest Publishing
c/o Pathway Book Service
P.O. Box 89
Gilsum, NH 03448

Hawk's Nest
Publishing, LLC

Books for the Young and Young at Heart...

HawksNestPublishing.com